TWENTY 4

JASMINE GABRIEL

ISBN-13: 9781790937738

DEDICATION

For you, Love

CONTENTS

ACKNOWLEDGMENTS

First and foremost I give thanks to God for blessing me with all of the wisdom, inspiration, and creativity I am able to share and inspire others with. I am honored you have chosen me to carry such love.

Deepest gratitude to my mother for being a humbling and compassionate force in my life. I'm so glad I chose you.

TO MY READERS

This collection of poetry is a reflection of the journey leading up to my twenty-fourth revolution around the Sun. TWENTY 4 is a celebration of healing, discovery, evolution, love of self, and living your highest potential.

I encourage you to read with heightened awareness of your initial reactions to each and every passage.

Throughout the poems I've included twenty-four invitations for you to consider your thoughts and emotions as you reflect on the words you read.

I intend for this for poetic journal to be a safe space for you to open your heart, explore what lives inside, and discover thyself cosmically.

May you accept with an open soul.

TWENTY 4

INCARNATION

a seed has been planted
bound to grow exponentially
but the process mustn't be rushed
Her soul can only take so much

all that is left behind
on Her own she must find
in the most challenging game of all
there are no winners or losers
only those
who've come to evolve

lying in the depths of Her mother's womb
the seed is nourished
love, warmth, and protection comfort Her
incredible beauty
this nurturing room

expanding Her reach
the flower has blossomed
she is becoming love
the aura of her petals
radiates divinity from above

Her light guides
the path of evolution
the soul will certainly flourish
a delicate jasmine
she dwells with purpose
divine love
she has become

EMERGENCE

I AM who the light must find
the quest is not without difficulty
to some my motivation is a crime
because my love for Her paints me
as villain and vigilante

when I emerge
the world gasps in astonishment
as if I was meant to stay hidden
content to live my life alone and anonymous

this here is my declaration
I cast away my shadow
with unlimited selfish vain

I AM the ego
underneath, above, and between the child
you know me now
hear my pain

PRISTINE

Her immaculateness
so innocently bound
and one of a kind
gave Her freedom
to speak what she felt
to feel what she knew
to know what it was like
to love and live her truth

FIRST CRUSH, THEN CRUSHED

the first time Her heart
fluttered from the piercing
of cupid's arrow
she grew with wonder
as to how Her enormous love
could grow any greater

as the infatuation expanded
so did Her chest
with hope
that Her love could be reciprocated
butterflies danced in Her belly
every time she laid eyes on
Her blossoming crush

little did she know
that flower was already tainted
his stem and leaves
tarnished with mildew
from the cries of his ancestors
who suffered under the hands
of pale colored hatred
that blinded him
from seeing beyond
the hue of Her petals

and so
with sightless eyes
he set his vision upon Her
his gaze emoted naïve disgust
indeed she disintegrated
into shameful dust

and it was there
at that heartbreaking moment
Her own reflection
became Her enemy
and Her redemption

somehow I found
deliverance
in the midst of
foggy perceptions
they call it the
law of attraction
I call it
kismet

those moments
when I remember
memories from my
future
I glow
with gratitude at the
realization that
I am always where
I'm meant
to be
presently

When the dots of your life connect
the complex design of
everything reveals a transcendant
beauty.
What constellations have you
mapped within your
life?

I

I allowed Her into
me to guide me
toward the
path of
holistic bliss

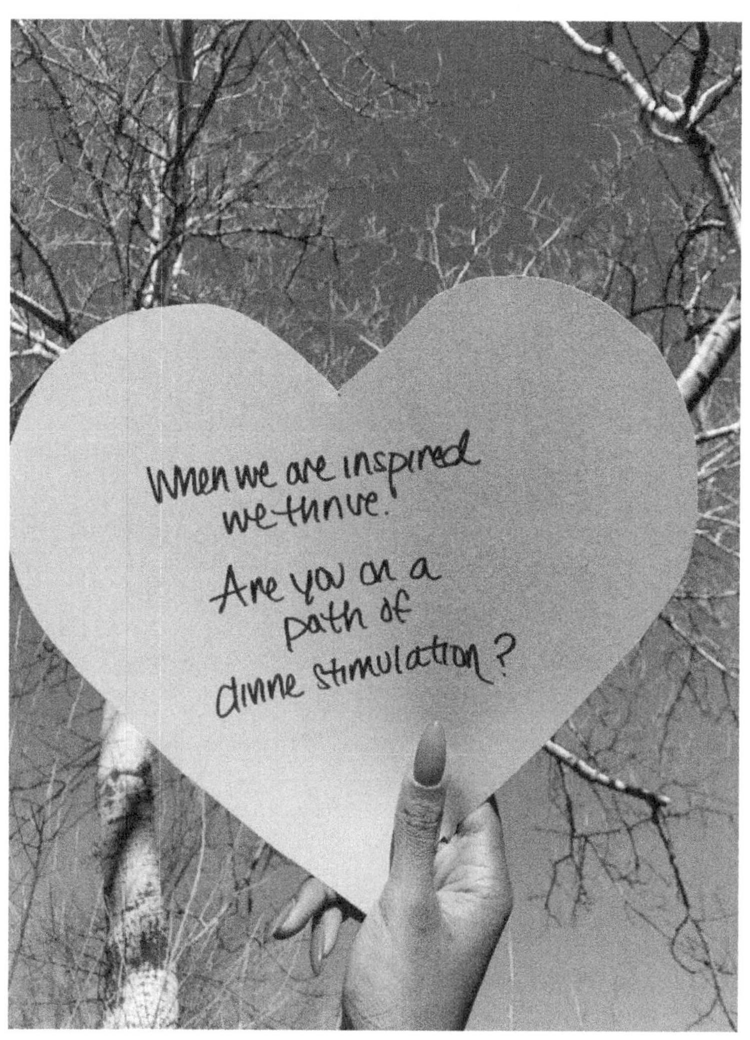
When we are inspired
we thrive.
Are you on a
path of
divine stimulation?

II

she moves
effortlessly
when she
expands with
divine
manipulation

How do you let
love
move you?

III

How do you let
fear
immobilise you?

IV

TWENTY 4

all through Her
journey
dandelions sprouted
whenever she
fell to the ground

The acidic soil still
offers flexibility.
How do you bounce
back from
adversity?

V

it took awhile
for my shame
to tell me
that she
mourns
not asking
for more
love

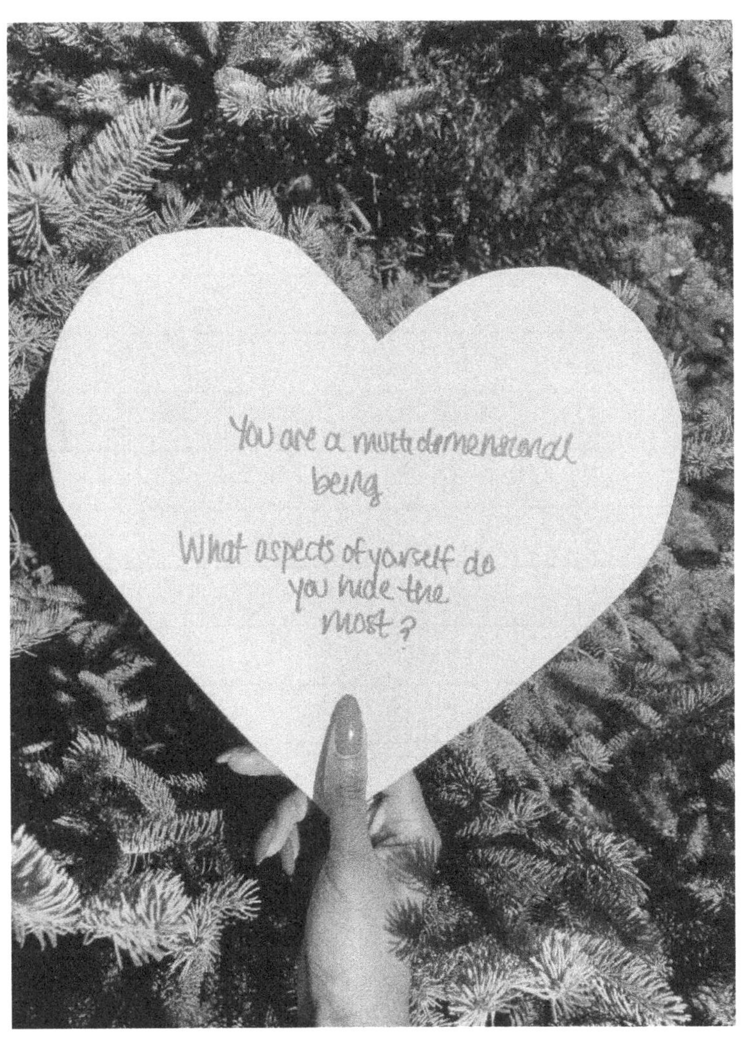
You are a multidimensional
being
What aspects of yourself do
you hide the
most?

VI

TWENTY 4

her self-worth
developed from a
foundation of ignorance
thus she seeks knowledge
for empowerment

limitation
is the belief
of impossibility
because what's
possible is
unbelievable

TWENTY 4

what am I
writing ?

love in full effect

I used to fear
my own
existence
until I asked for
courage to love
myself in every way
that I AM

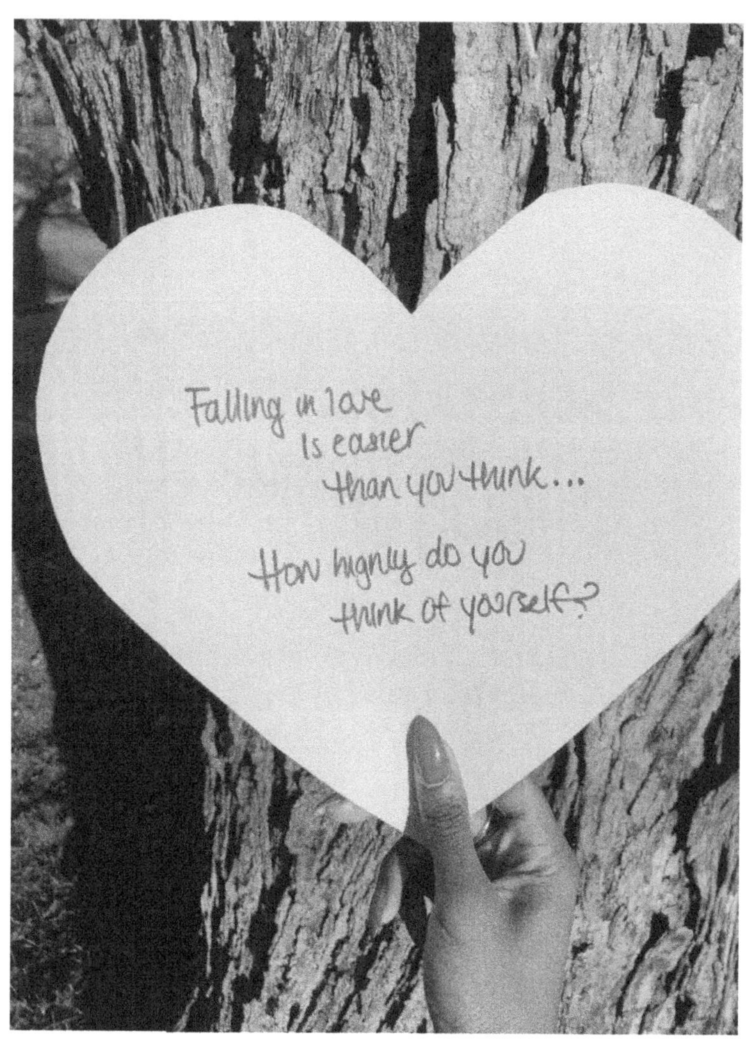
Falling in love
is easier
than you think...
How highly do you
think of yourself?

VII

lay down unto me
your pink flame
let the heat
ignite and blaze
so hot it turns
blue
enveloping me
in the hottest ocean
full of love and
truth

where the current
travels without
turbulent streams
of falsehood
the vessel becomes a
container for
truth to live
among
serenity

Going with the flow
of your life
pulls you to your destiny.
Are you pushing
against fate?

VIII

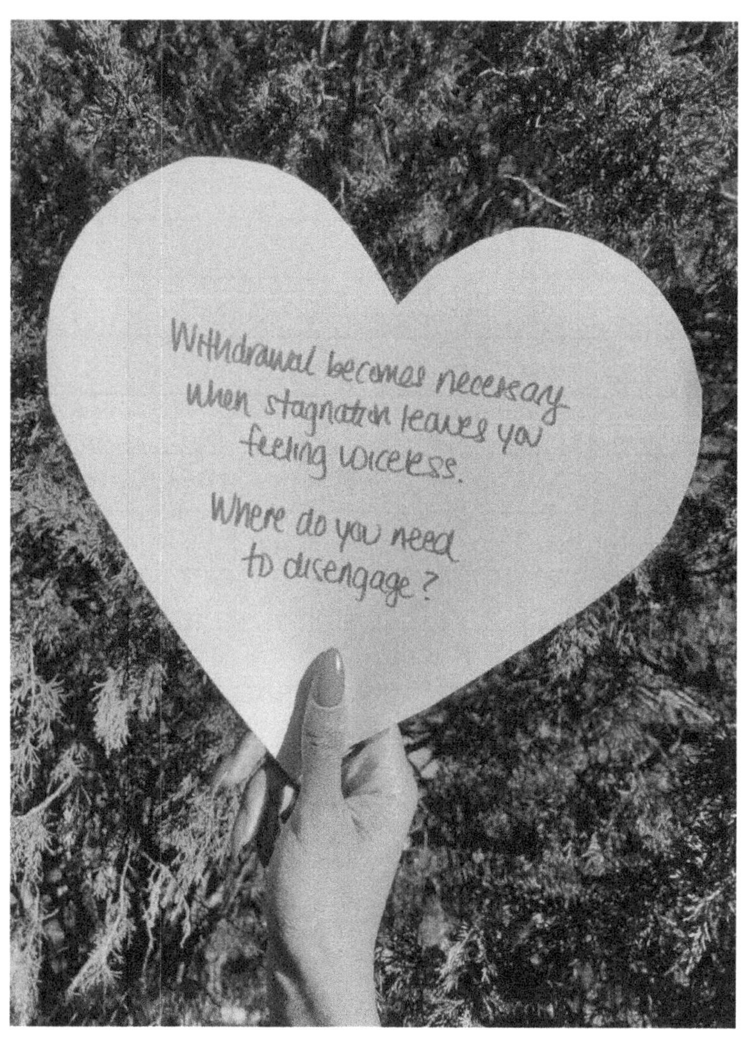
Withdrawal becomes necessary
when stagnation leaves you
feeling voiceless.
Where do you need
to disengage?

IX

silence became my solace
when it whispered
to me it could
hear all of my
secrets

"my space is
self-governed
every corner
has its
destiny
fulfilled"

"my soul sings
a frequency
that relates
with the curiosity
of your potential"

TWENTY 4

"my point of view
glares with
a clarity
rivaling that of the tip of a
herkimer diamond
therefore
I AM
all seeing"

"my heart now bulbous
with
the smoke of love
prospers into
every one of my
cells that
breathes
yearning"

"I resent my own guilt-
when I question
my gift to feel everything:
is it a blessing,
is it a curse,

can I bear them both?"

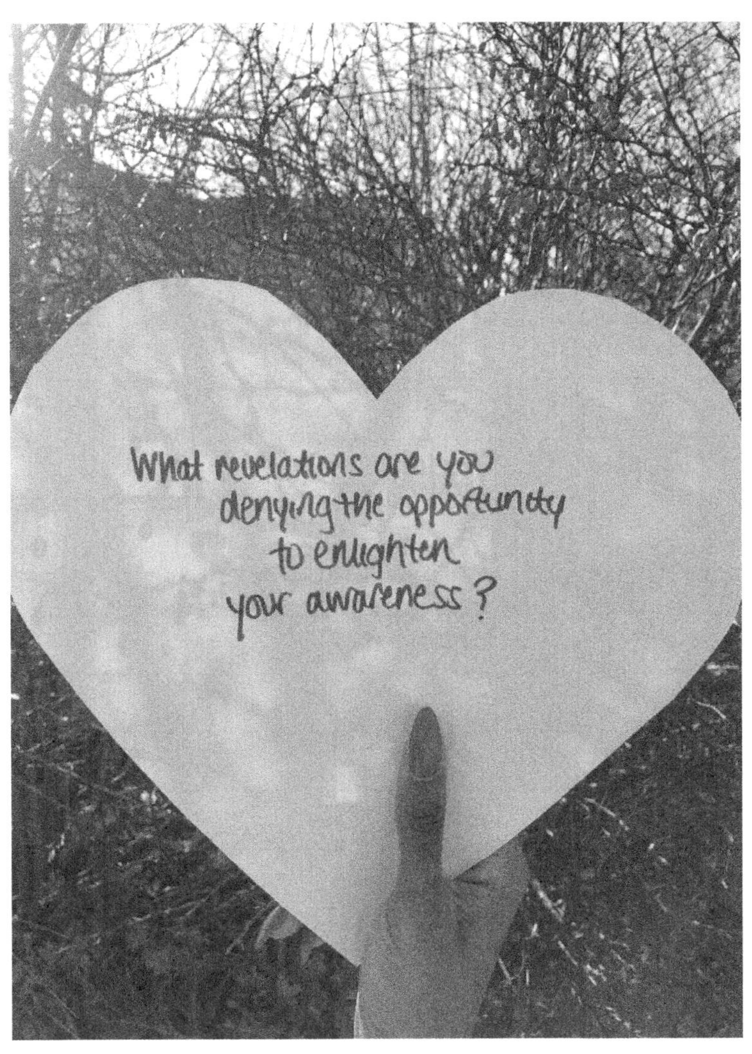
What revelations are you
denying the opportunity
to enlighten
your awareness?

X

TWENTY 4

a piece of paper
once showed me
the chain I
had around my heart

in actuality I saw
my fingerprints
reflected on a
fairytale
of
denial

depression is
only possible
with disbelief
of your
greatness

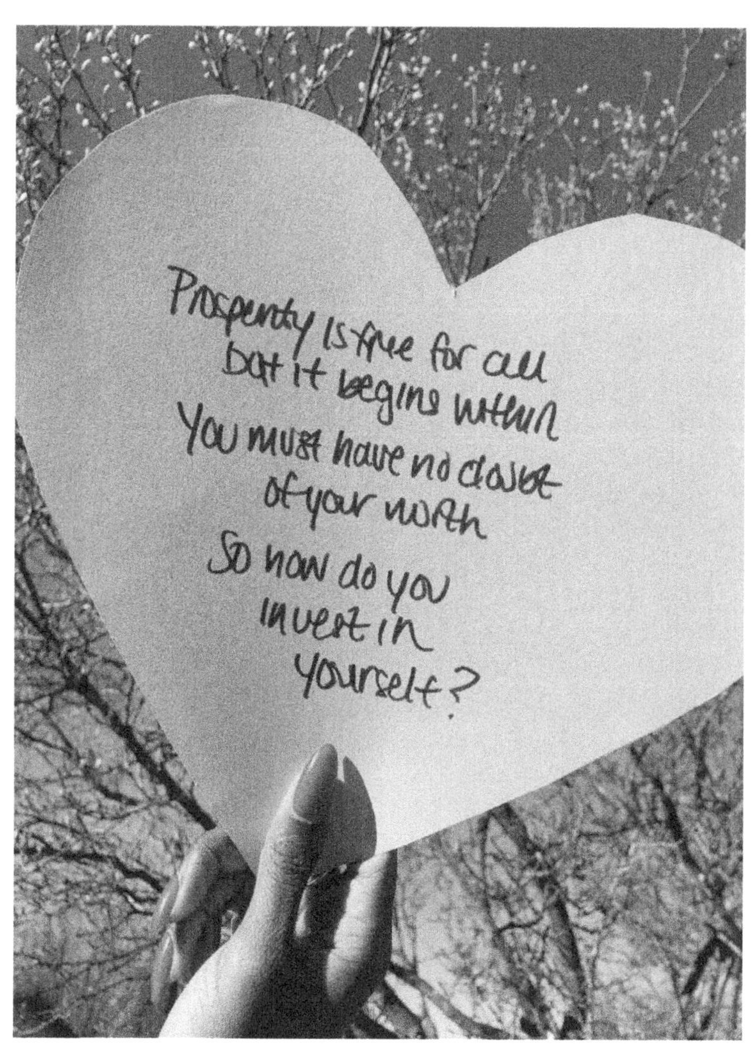
Prosperity is free for all
but it begins within
You must have no doubt
of your worth
So how do you
invest in
yourself?

XI

polarities blind you
from embracing
love's shadow

where your demons
lie
underneath
the heavy black hooves
rooted in your attachments
that protect you from pain
purposely waiting
for you to overcome
your fear

look into your abyss
and love what appears

TWENTY 4

I never noticed
how blue the sky is
a distinct hue of revelation

the kind of blue
that never fades
only becomes richer
and richer
the more you gaze

the kind of blue
that caresses the rods
and cones behind
the eye

the kind that makes you wonder
how long have I
been living in dullness,
on standby?

What do you feel
when you see
your
mirrored
image?

XII

TWENTY 4

the spine

is
the
vertical
access
to
all
that
exists

Where do you
feel out of
alignment?

XIII

TWENTY 4

happiness is
harmony with
what is

How can you create
synergy
with your
conflicts?

XIV

TWENTY 4

lakes turn into
oceans when
they arouse
the universe
to fulfill
them
with all
they can be

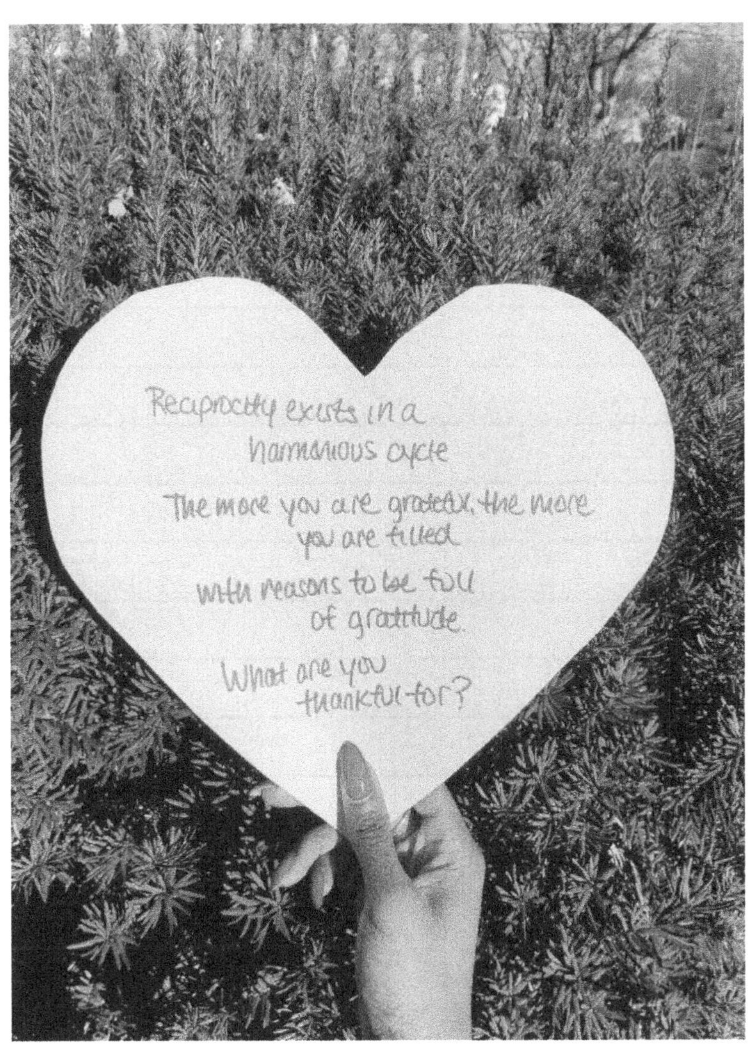
Reciprocity exists in a
harmonious cycle
The more you are grateful, the more
you are filled
with reasons to be full
of gratitude.
What are you
thankful for?

XV

TWENTY 4

how can one describe
the essence of everything
in a reality
that fears
knowing its
own self

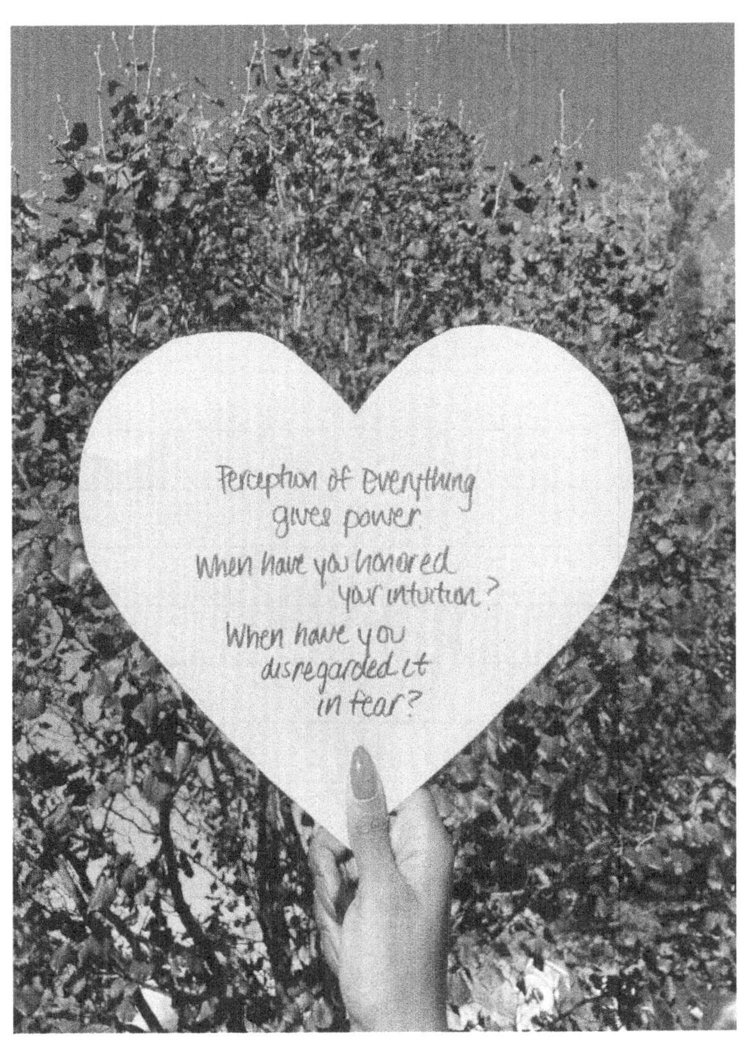
Perception of Everything
gives power.
When have you honored
your intuition?
When have you
disregarded it
in fear?

XVI

there is a war that
begins before
birth
for the gift
of humanity:
welcome your
tribulations

I hope this
awareness of
possibility
entrances you to
never stop
digging
deep
into your scars for
you will find healing
obscured below the
violent consequence
of
reopening
old
wounds

VENUS

all of the women
the media broadcasts
share the same shades and tints
words of beauty
bestowed upon them repetitively
they become
the representative of
glamour and ideal femininity

I sit humbly on the floor
then look down
at my thighs
and begin to realize
the incongruency
my pigment doesn't match
the standard currency
I guess that means
I must be ugly

my trembling hands
caress my skin
with this new perspective
I gaze upon what appears to be
a stain and a sin

I become fearful of my future
because my blush
makes me a target
for the other children
who are conduits for self-contempt

their pain manifests
as lightning bolted words
sent with the intention
to release their agony
upon those who only mirror themselves

I wonder of a wish
to be a different color
maybe if I scratch hard enough
the scabs will lift to reveal something duller

the devastation settles in then
from the realization
that I am stuck forever
in this complex complexion

TWENTY 4

I open
so I grow

I put all of my
reluctance
into one basket
and burned it
till I no longer
struggled
to be myself
authentically

Focus on your breath
for a moment.
Feel the beat of your heart
in sync with the expansion
of your heart.
Listen.
What is it
singing to
you?

XVII

I did not expect
to be dwelling
in this much
promise
may I
develop to
absolute capacity

How do you protect
yourself from
negativity
that diminishes
your power?

XVIII

I've burned out
      enough

to know
   that

my light
      never
      goes out

TWENTY 4

you only have to
let all that
you are be expressed
free of the
egotistical
confines
you
trap
yourself
in

When our hearts ignite
It burns through
any obstacle.
What sets your
heart on fire?

XIX

my heart broke
under the weight
of unwept tears
guarded by the well
of my suffering
I AM lighter now
I AM free
waiting for the next
wave to swell
surrender
and let me be

I look back
at my pains with
rose colored irises
so that my vision
only sees the
divine purpose

I finally
stopped holding on
to the magnet
that brought me
nothing but
division

cords are valuable until
they fulfill their purpose.
What bonds are you
holding affection for
that no longer
serves you?

XX

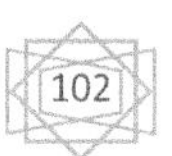
102

now one can hear the pitter patter
of the ego
running free
in nothing can
ever dilute
Her selfish love

We are our own
children.
How do you
raise yourself?

XXI

why carry worry for the
end of time
when you
are beyond
third dimensional
construction

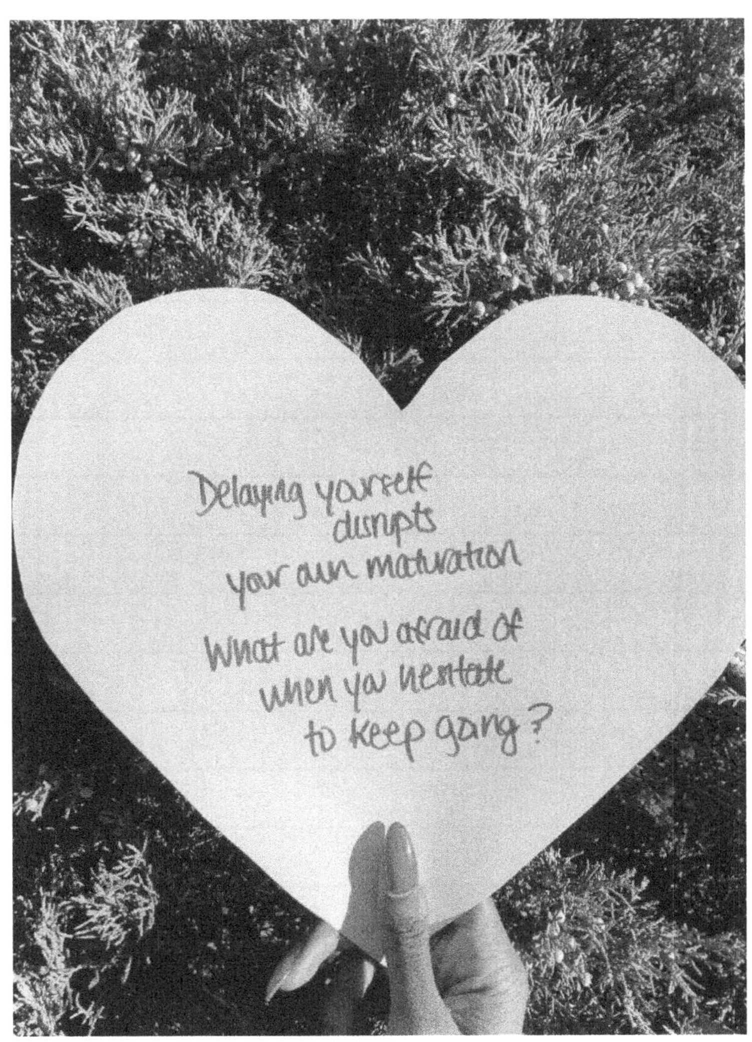
Delaying yourself
disrupts
your own maturation
What are you afraid of
when you hesitate
to keep going?

XXII

every little ripple.
you hesitate to make
sounds like the
absence of life

I wish you could
feel the
euphoric friction
I create as
I rake
my fingers
through what cynics deny
to be my
crowning glory

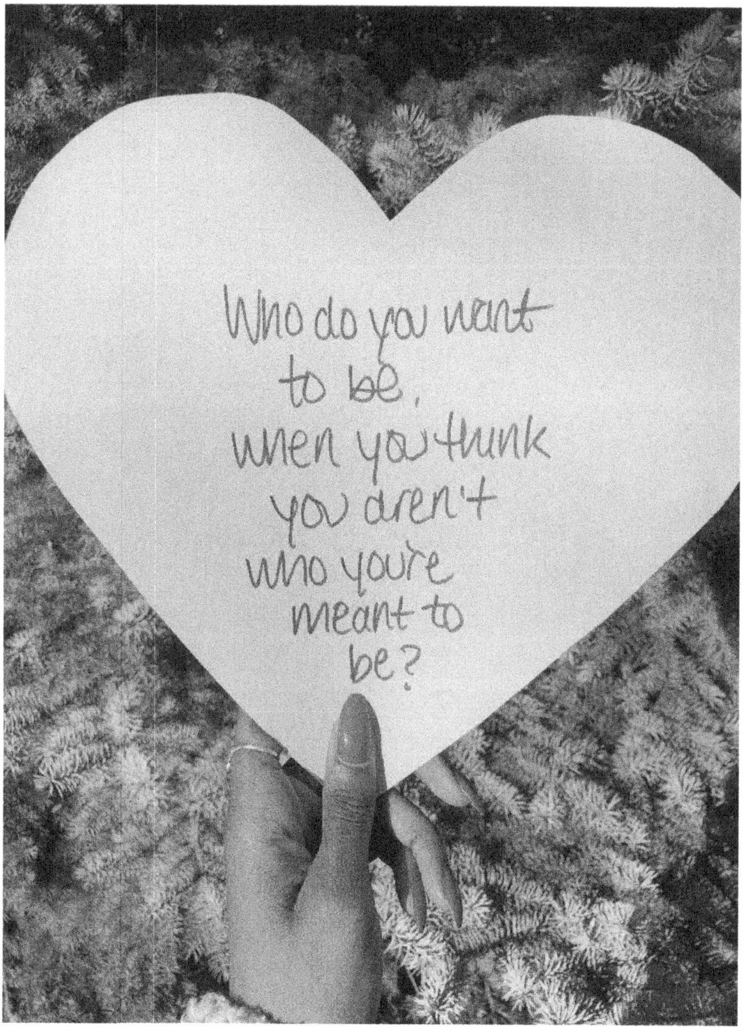

Who do you want
to be,
when you think
you aren't
who you're
meant to
be?

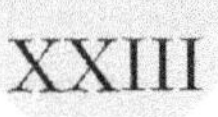

XXIII

bless
heal
love
she says

She said
Amen

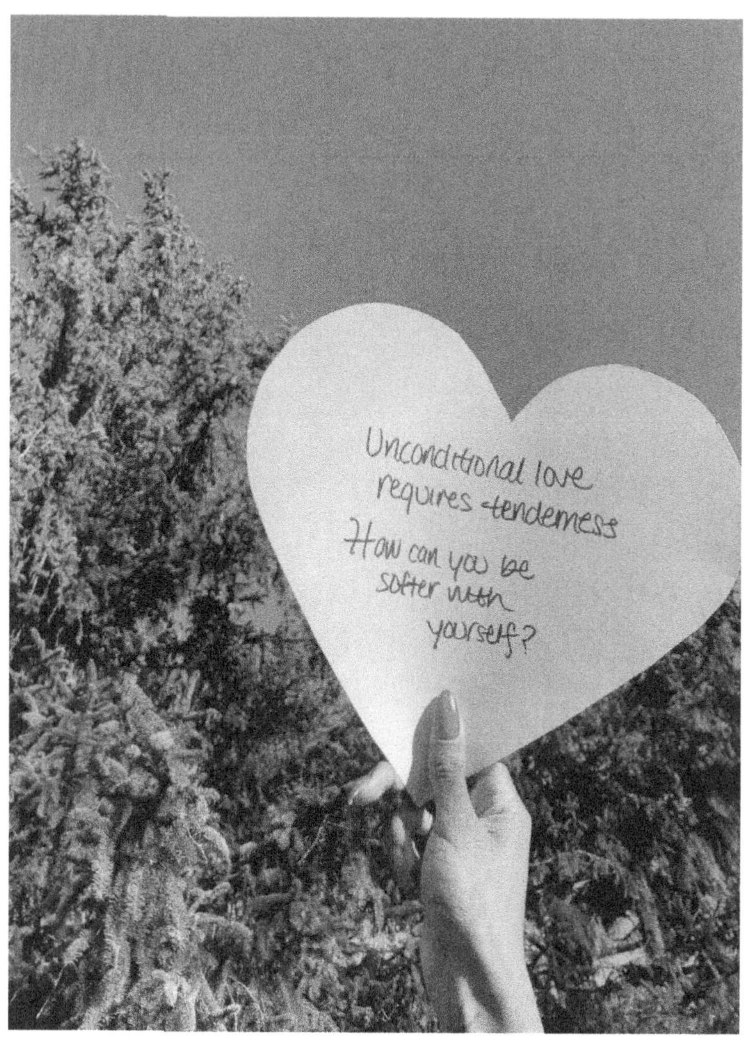
Unconditional love
requires tenderness
How can you be
softer with
yourself?

XXIV

120

from here I Kreate
my own path
in this way
my journey lacks
resistance
the destination seeks my
company
and we find each other
in the greatest
discovery:

s e p a r a t i o n   i s   an illusion

embrace your
flaws and imperfections
until love of self
is effortless

I've surrendered
now I've grown

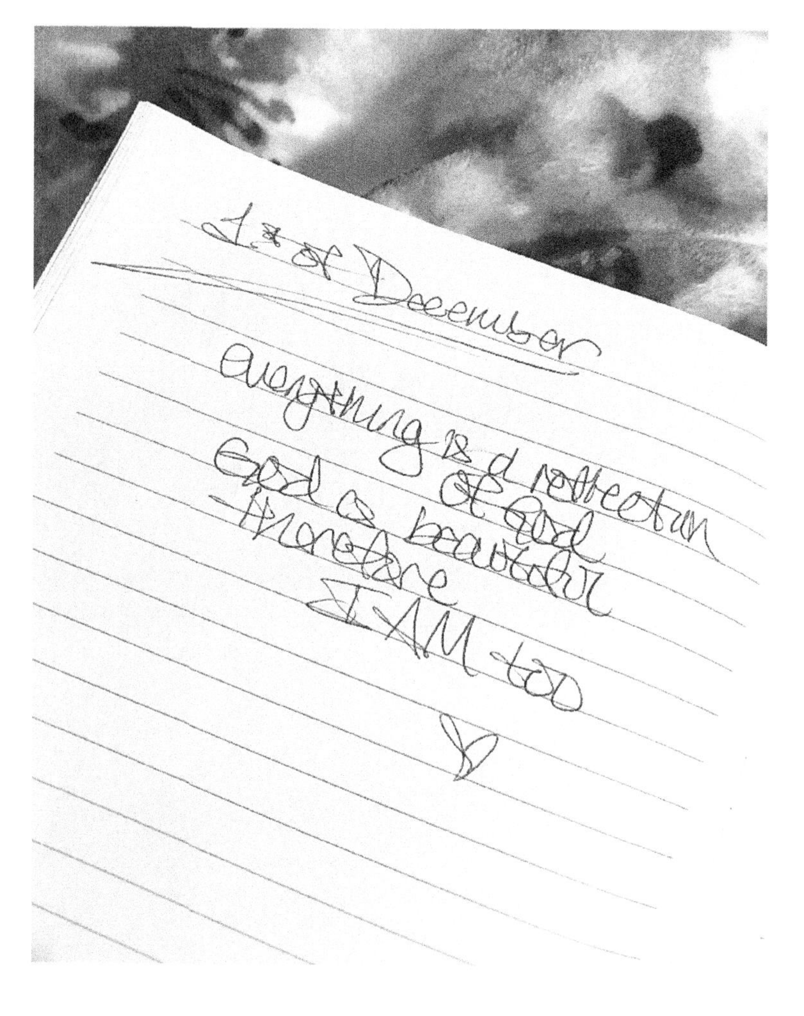
1st of December
everything is a reflection
of God
God is beautiful
therefore
I AM too

ABOUT THE AUTHOR

Archangel Jasmine enchanted with all things Divine, writes to open portals for Spirit to dance among us in the physical realm. A lover of angels, elementals, and the big blue, she intends that her art heals the soul of all enraptured hearts.

Made in the USA
Monee, IL
28 January 2023